LOVE
YOUR LIFE
On Planet Earth

*A Guide To Recognising
Your True Self*

VIMLA RAO

First published in Australia by Vimla Rao

This edition published 2024
Copyright © Vimla Rao 2024

Typesetting and e-book design: Amit Dey (amitdey2528@gmail.com)
Cover Designer: Vimla Rao/Donika Mishineva (www.artofdonika.com)

The right of Vimla Rao to be identified as Author of the Work has been asserted in accordance with the Copyright, Designs and Patents Act 1988.

ISBN number: 978-1-925471-64-9 (paperback)

All rights reserved. No part of this publication may be reproduced, stored in a retrieval system, or transmitted, in any form or by any means without the prior written permission of the publisher, nor be otherwise circulated in any form of binding or cover other than that in which it is published and without a similar condition being imposed on the subsequent purchaser.

 A catalogue record for this book is available from the National Library of Australia

Distributed by: Ingram Content, www.ingramcontent.com
Australia: phone +613 9765 4800 | email lsiaustralia@ingramcontent.com
Milton Keynes UK: phone +44 (0)845 121 4567 | email enquiries@ingramcontent.com
La Vergne, TN USA: phone +1 800 509 4156 | email inquiry@lightningsource.com

DISCLAIMER

This book aims to share insights about self-discovery and the Source based on the author's personal experiences. The views and opinions expressed are solely those of the author and may not represent those of any religious or spiritual organization.

The book is not intended to replace professional advice, such as medical or psychological guidance. If you have any health or mental health issues, please consult a qualified professional. The practices in this book may not be suitable for everyone.

The author and publisher are not liable for any consequences arising from the use of the information in this book. By choosing to read it, you acknowledge that you're responsible for your own decisions and well-being.

DEDICATION

To the Divine Source, my silent Helper, whose wisdom and guidance light the path.

To my family, for their unconditional love and support.

And to all the seekers, may you find peace and enlightenment on your journey.

With gratitude from the core of my heart,

Vimla Rao

CONTENTS

Intention Prayer: To Be One with The Divine Energy/ Universal Consciousness		ix
Author's Note		xi
Preface		xv
Hierarchy of the Various States of Human Life on Planet Earth:		xvii
1	Human Life	1
2	Love and Happiness: The True Nature of the Self	5
3	Love: The Light That Shines Within	7
4	Happiness: The Continuous Search	11
5	The Five Basic Elements: Earth, Water, Fire, Air, and Ether	13
6	The Human Body: The Physical/Gross Body	19
7	Humanity: Universal Kindness	21
8	The Spirit the Soul and the Ultimate Source (The Divine)	23
9	Spirituality	29
10	The Soul	33
11	Who Am I? The Body, the Spirit, or the Soul?	37

12	The Divine Energy: The Source of all Creation	41
13	Divinity: Living in Oneness	45
14	Ocean of Love and Happiness	47
15	Surrender: Embracing The Ocean (The Source) and Letting Go	51
16	Selfless Service: The Ultimate Expression of Love and Happiness	57
17	Change Your Mindset: Be One with the Ocean of Love and Happiness	61
18	Silence as a Gateway to the Divine	67
Conclusion		71
Acknowledgements		73
About the Author		75

Intention Prayer

TO BE ONE WITH THE DIVINE ENERGY/ UNIVERSAL CONSCIOUSNESS

Divine Presence, Source of all creation, of this universe and beyond
I bow before you with a humble and open heart.
I seek to know, understand, and embrace Your infinite energy,
To become one with the divine essence that pervades all, living and non-living.

Please help me release all that holds me back, All doubts, fears, and limitations.
And open my being to the flow of Your Divine love, knowledge, and wisdom,
Allow me to recognize that it is your essence that pervades my entire being.

Guide me to walk the path of being one with infinite consciousness.
Let me love every moment of my life on planet earth.
May I feel Your presence in every moment,
And recognize the divine nature of myself and all others.

Help me to act with love and kindness,
To serve with a pure heart,
And to live in harmony with Your divine will.
May my actions reflect Your grace and goodness,
Bringing peace and joy to the world around me.

I most humbly request for the wisdom to stay one with You,
Even in times of challenge and uncertainty.
Let The divinity flow through my entire being,
Healing and transforming back to my true nature,
And guiding me to my highest purpose.

I am grateful for Your constant presence, love, and mercy.
I trust in Your infinite wisdom and Divine plan.
I surrender to Your will and your wishes,
Knowing that in Your embrace, I am complete and one with thee.
With deep reverence and gratitude,
I offer this prayer.

May I always be one with and surrendered to Your Divine Essence, the Source, that pervades all living and non-living, now and forevermore.

AUTHOR'S NOTE

Writing *Love Your Life on Planet Earth* has been a deeply personal journey, inspired by a desire to dive deeper into the Ocean of Love and Happiness, knowledge, and wisdom, while living as a householder and to help others do the same.

As a therapist and instructor of Bowen Therapy and spiritual hypnotherapy, I've encountered many clients and students who've suffered from unresolved traumas, leading them to perceive life on Earth as miserable. Witnessing their struggles with depression, anxiety, and suicidal thoughts inspired me to share the knowledge and wisdom I've gained from my personal journey. Like my clients and students, I've faced intense personal traumas and hardships that left me struggling to find happiness.

From a young age, I endured harshness, sexual trauma, neglect, and disownment. My marriage and becoming an unmarried mother led me to being labelled a disgrace by my family and society. For several months, my husband, my child, and I lived in isolation and poverty, until I was offered a position as a technical officer at the University of the South Pacific. This opportunity marked a turning point in my life, allowing me to re-join society as a giver, rather than just a receiver.

After twenty years of navigating the complexities of married life, I once again faced isolation and disownment when my husband took his own life. These were dark moments, but they ultimately led me to my spiritual master, who initiated me into spirituality.

On February 18, 2002, six months after my husband took his own life, I was initiated into the path of spirituality. Almost immediately, I felt no need to search for the ultimate Truth any longer. To my surprise, the void left by my loss was filled by the presence of divine energy. I began to realise that I always had an invisible helper with me. My entire being transformed. Questions, doubts, blame, and regrets faded away. I came to understand that death is simply another phase in one's journey.

The words of my spiritual master remain vivid in my mind, fundamentally shifting my perspective. He said, "When a person is born, their journey on this planet is already planned. All major events in life, such as their parents, spouse, children, education, wealth, family, friends, and the circumstances of their death, are predetermined. The higher self and nature play their roles to ensure these planned incidents occur." He further added, "However, one is also given free will, which can be used to change one's mindset and modify the pre-planned journey to their advantage."

During his discourses, he often spoke of surrender and the motherly love of the Divine source. In my desperation to find love and happiness, I embraced his teachings and relinquished the rituals and religious practices that had been ingrained in me.

Through the practices of chanting and meditation, I realised that we're always one with the Source. Our misery stems from ignorance, failing to recognise our connection to the Source of all creation, living and non-living, including health, wealth, and our desires. All we need is to shift our mindset and embrace this divine connection.

My personal journey has brought me to a state of surrender, where all my needs and wants are fulfilled.

Surrounded by my biological family, friends, students, clients, and the communities I serve, I feel like the happiest person on Earth. I have no reason to be depressed or anxious. Solutions to unforeseen issues often present themselves before they even arise. The happiness and love that surround me are beyond words.

As I navigated the ups and downs of my personal life, I discovered that our planet offers not only breathtaking beauty, but also lessons in resilience, hope, and love. This book reflects my experiences and learnings, aiming to encourage readers to appreciate the wonders of our world and to find joy and meaning in every moment. My hope is that these pages will serve as a guide to embracing life with an open heart and a renewed sense of purpose.

PREFACE

In the grand tapestry of the universe, while each of us is unique, we're woven together by the delicate hands of fate and the infinite source of all creation. As we navigate our journeys on this vibrant planet, we often seek meaning, connection, and a deeper understanding of our purpose. Love Your Life on Planet Earth is based on personal experience and an exploration of these aspects, guided by the profound wisdom of Oneness with the Source.

This book is an invitation to reconnect with the essence of who we truly are and to embrace the boundless love that surrounds us. It's a gentle reminder that despite the challenges and uncertainties we face, we're never alone. The Universe, in its infinite kindness, offers us countless opportunities grow and transform.

The connection between humanity, spirituality, and divinity is like a journey that brings deeper meaning to our lives. As humans, we often seek a sense of purpose and understanding beyond our everyday experiences. Spirituality helps us find this by connecting us to something greater than ourselves. It's like a bridge that leads us to a feeling of being part of the larger universe. It then leads to the feeling that's often called divinity. It's the sense that there's a higher power or a universal force guiding us.

By utilising tools like meditation, prayer, and reflection, we can tap into this divine source, finding guidance and a sense of belonging.

In this way, our human experiences and connection to the Divine come together, helping us grow and feel more connected to everything within and around us.

Embracing the Divine Source results in being one with it. However, while on earth in the human body with desires and purpose, you need to surrender to the Source of all creations to lead a life full of love and happiness that results in everlasting contentment.

As you turn these pages, allow yourself to be open to the transformative power of love and oneness. Embrace the lessons and insights offered, and let them guide you toward a life of greater fulfillment and peace. Remember, you're a cherished part of this magnificent universe, and your journey is a vital contribution to the collective whole.

May this book serve as an inspiration of light on your path, illuminating the way to a deeper connection with not only yourself and others, but the Source of all creation. Together, let us celebrate the gift of life on this beautiful planet and cherish the love that binds us all.

With infinite love and gratitude,
Oneness with the Source

HIERARCHY OF THE VARIOUS STATES OF HUMAN LIFE ON PLANET EARTH:

The hierarchy of human life can be seen as a journey from the tangible to the transcendental, beginning with the human body.

1. The Body

The body is our physical vessel, a complex organism of flesh and bone that grounds us in the material world. It enables us to experience and interact with our environment. Rising from the individual body, we encounter humanity, the collective experience of human beings.

The Body emphasises our social nature, connections, relationships, and the shared culture and history that bind us together.

2. Humanity

Humanity is at a physical and material level and includes traits like kindness, empathy, and the ability to love and understand each other. Despite our differences, humanity aims to improve the world through curiosity and learning. At its heart, it's where everyone's value and potential are appreciated and supported.

At the level of Humanity, we work hard to fulfill our needs and desires.

3. Spirituality

Beyond Humanity lies Spirituality, where the focus shifts from external connections to internal exploration. It's directly related to the Spirit, meaning the energetic aspects of the being. Spirituality involves seeking deeper meaning, understanding our place in the Universe, and nurturing the soul. It's a quest for enlightenment and focuses on our journey and experiences.

Spirituality can be expressed in various ways, such as meditation, mindfulness, nature walks, yoga, and other personal practices that promote a sense of well-being and connection with our inner self. Spirituality encourages oneness with the Universe and all that exists.

At the Spiritual level, we use methods and tools to fulfill our needs and desires.

4. Divinity

Higher still is Divinity, the recognition of a higher power or the Divine essence within and beyond us. Divinity is directly associated with the Soul. This level transcends individual and collective existence, aspiring to connect with the ultimate source of life and creation of all existence. It aims at knowing our true nature by understanding, and embracing the Source. Its goal is to be one with the Supreme, the Universal.

Consciousness. Once the self and the Divine Source is understood and accepted, we can then recognise that the relationship between them is the same as the ocean and the wave.

Divinity encourages oneness with the Divine Source, which encompasses the Universe and beyond.

At the Divinity level, we recognize and embrace oneness and feel that everything simply IS. In the stillness of existence, there is no separation. The duality diminishes.

5. Surrender

Finally, Surrender represents the culmination of this journey. It's the act of letting go, trusting in the Divine Order, and merging the individual self with the greater whole. Surrender is an acceptance of the mysteries of life and a profound union with the Divine, achieving a state of ultimate peace and oneness. At the level of Surrender, we recognize that while on planet Earth, they are three in one: the body, the spirit, and the soul.

This is the true nature of existence. Everything in the Universe simply is, united in oneness, with the physical, mental, and emotional aspects of everyone still existing, each with its own unique needs and desires. These aspects of our human experience call for fulfillment, drawing us into the dance of life.

To fully embrace this quest, we must surrender to the Source of all creation, the infinite wellspring from which everything arises. In this Surrender, we find peace, allowing us to fully enjoy and appreciate the beauty of life while inhabiting our human form. Through this balance, we honor both our individuality and our connection to the greater whole.

Once Surrendered, we find joy in serving the creations of the Source, and the Source serves us with an abundance of Love.

Divinity Versus Spirituality

These concepts are often intertwined and interchanged but in fact are distinct in their meanings and implications, in the same way spirit and soul are lumped together due to lack of clarity. Many people find their spiritual experiences enriched by their beliefs in Divinity, and conversely, their understanding of Divinity deepened by their spiritual practices.

In our shared humanity, we find our way, Through spirituality, our spirits sway. With Divine grace, our lives intertwine, In love and unity, we forever shine.

1

HUMAN LIFE

Each dawn that breaks, a chance anew,
To seek the path, to find the true.
With love as compass, faith as guide, In
human life, we take the ride.

Human life is rich and multifaceted, complex and unique in nature.

Humans are often considered the highest or most advanced species in the animal kingdom due to a combination of cognitive, social, and technological achievements that distinguish them from other animals.

While animals exhibit behaviours that can be seen as empathetic, ritualistic, or socially bonding, these behaviours are generally driven by instinct and immediate practical needs, rather than spiritual contemplation or belief. Human spirituality, on the other hand, involves complex abstract thinking, self-awareness, existential reflection, and the creation of religious and spiritual systems. This quest for connection with a higher reality or deeper truth is a defining aspect of human existence and sets humans apart from other animals in the realm of spirituality.

However, other species have their own unique and remarkable adaptations that enable them to thrive in their respective environments.

Human life, the soul, and the spirit are intricately connected, each playing a vital role in our overall existence. By nurturing our physical health, embracing our soulful emotions, and cultivating our spiritual connection, we can achieve a harmonious and fulfilling life. This holistic approach not only enhances our personal well-being but also deepens our understanding of the interconnected nature of all life, guiding us toward a more compassionate and enlightened way of being.

Our Divinity, the highest attribute, serves not only mankind but also the Universe. Within and beyond the perception of the human eye is the source of the ocean of love and happiness. By merely knowing, understanding, and embracing this ultimate intrinsic knowledge, we can attain the love and happiness that would not only fulfil our needs but encourage us to love our life on planet Earth.

The four primary needs or goals of human life:

1. Fulfilling Our Duties

This includes duties toward ourselves, family, society, and the world, accepting our moral values, ethical duties, and righteousness. It refers to the path of living a life of adherence to ethical principles. To be able to fulfill these duties, we need wealth and prosperity.

2. Wealth or Prosperity

This is about providing for ourselves, our family, and beyond, achieving economic stability and accumulating the means necessary to live a comfortable life. Career and professional goals are the necessary elements required to prosper and attain enough wealth to fulfil our duties.

3. Pleasure or Desires

Joy and satisfaction come through fulfilled desires and pleasures in life. This includes the physical, sensual, emotional, and spiritual. Other pleasures such as love, art, music, and other forms of personal fulfilment encourages joy and satisfaction.

Fulfillment of these pleasures enhances the love and happiness we desire for ourselves and loved ones.

4. Freedom (Liberation or Salvation)

The need for freedom is a fundamental aspect of human life. It's deeply rooted in the human psyche.

Freedom at a Physical level means being unburdened from life's miseries, aches, and pains. Freedom allows us to express ourselves fully, whether through speech, art, or lifestyle choices, which fosters a sense of control and responsibility that's essential for personal growth and self-fulfilment.

At a Spiritual level, we seek freedom from karma accumulation and the cycle of birth and Death. It's the calling of the individual spirit that encourages us to search for different tools of spirituality.

At the Soul level it's all about freedom from the encasement of the Ego.

Even after achieving freedom from the cycle of birth and death, the Ego keeps us rooted in our individuality in the higher levels of the spiritual world. It's only after shedding the Ego that we attain the ultimate oneness with the Source. This is when the Drop merges with the ocean and losses its identity.

2

LOVE AND HAPPINESS: THE TRUE NATURE OF THE SELF

Where love resides, happiness thrives,
together we soar, our spirits alive.

Happiness manifests in love, and love initiates happiness.

Love and Happiness intertwine and reinforce each other. The presence of love indicates happiness in life. Love and happiness initiate the health and wellbeing of the individual, families' societies, countries, and most of all, planet Earth.

Each one of us is searching for happiness and love.

Are we searching for Love and Happiness in the right places?

Once there lived a wise woman in a village. Her name was Rabia, but everyone called her "mother." Rabia was old but full of knowledge and wisdom, and loved all in the village without exception.

Most evenings the villagers would gather around her to listen to stories and receive guidance.

One day, the villagers saw Rabia outside searching for a needle she'd lost. Very soon, they joined in her search.

After a while, one of them asked: "Mother, where exactly did you drop the needle?"

"Inside in my room," said Rabia.

The young man laughed and said, "Then you should look for the needle inside."

"It's dark inside my room," Rabia said.

"Mother," he said, "Let's take a torch and look for the needle inside. You shall never find the needle out here."

Rabia smiled and said, "Yes, my son. This is exactly what I've been trying to explain to you. The source of love and happiness resides within you, but due to your darkness of ignorance, you're searching for it in the material world. How can you find outside that which resides within?"

For the source to be revealed within, we need to move from Ignorance to Knowledge.

Ignorance lies in not knowing the True Nature of oneself.

Knowledge is the understanding of being One with the Source, the Divine Energy.

3

LOVE: THE LIGHT
THAT SHINES WITHIN

With every step and every sigh,
We seek the love that lifts us high.

The greatest happiness in life is the conviction that you are loved despite who you are.

Love is beyond the perception of the five senses and is hard to define. But even though the nature of love is difficult to put into words, it's an emotion that has many facets and has been around since the beginning of civilization. Most people would agree that love implies strong feelings of affection and warmth, and can be for self or for others. It involves care, closeness, protectiveness, trust, affection, attraction, and a set of emotions and behaviours characterised by intimacy, passion, and commitment.

Love is the most essential Element of every being and is the greatest power in the world.

Research suggests even babies in the womb love when their mothers talk and stroke their bumps. It's believed that plants don't have nervous systems, but they respond to vibrations. The way you touch a plant and how you talk to them creates vibrations accordingly.

A loving and caring touch and tone makes plants thrive.

Love is a bond that often involves understanding each other's core values, beliefs and life goals. It fosters connections, working as a team, and goes beyond the superficial.

According to Buddhism, it's about unselfishly wishing others to be happy, offering our smiles and hugs, and helping freely without wanting anything in return. Love is feeling delighted in the presence of the one you love.

Each of us desires to receive and experience love. We seek it in all aspects of our life, and even in nature. But it resides within us, ready to be shared to others.

Love may come in different forms and expressed uniquely. Love for a child may be greater than love for your animal or your neighbor, but the meaning never diminishes.

Divine Love is received in the core of our beings, our soul. It's perfect and universal. It's toward all beings and creatures. Divine love is the feeling of oneness with the whole Universe and beyond.

To see yourself in everybody, and everybody in yourself, most certainly is Divine love. I personally believe in loving all without exception.

Love's the thread that binds us all,
A whispering truth, a gentle call.
It's the nature of our soul's own light,
A flame that burns forever bright.

Unconditional Love: The Divine Love
Through the ages, mystics, saints, singers, and poets have all expressed the uniqueness of unconditional love. It's the greatest power you're born with and remains a core of the inner self. It manifests as the umbilical cord through which the fetus receives all the nutrients from the mother and the milk in her breast, as well as her sleepless nights. It manifests as sacrifice and being a role model.

Unconditional love has no strings tied to it. You simply love and do not expect anything in return. All you wish for is the happiness of those you love. You're filled with happiness when you see them happy.

Love flows is like a river, flowing continuously through humble, sincere souls. Selfishness, anger, greed, and ego are like the rocks and blocks in the river that create hurdles.

It's the unconditional love that recognises the beauty in every moment.

Express love, and the world will reflect that power.

Unconditional love helps us to recognise our wholeness and oneness, and that we're interconnected. We transcend to the higher truth, the Divinity with in us.

Unconditional love, a boundless sea,
Embraces all, sets hearts free.
In the gentle touch of love's embrace,
We uncover the truth of divine grace.
No wealth or fame can claim this space,
Only a heart that finds its place.

4

HAPPINESS: THE CONTINUOUS SEARCH

In the quiet of the heart's deep sea,
Happiness whispers, "Come find me."

Happiness is a fundamental and essential need of human life, and each of us is unconsciously in search of it.

Happiness is a feeling that's unique to everyone. Typically, it's an emotional state that has many definitions but is often characterised by joy, satisfaction, and contentment. For me personally, happiness is a state that fills me with love, a need to hug those around me, being in acceptance, and perhaps also a feeling of total fulfilment.

Happiness is about creating harmony across all aspects of life. It involves managing and completing demands and finding a middle ground where various elements of well-being can coexist. Achieving this balance leads to a feeling of happiness, enhancing overall life satisfaction and resilience.

This joy helps lower levels of stress and anxiety and promotes a sense of calmness and stability.

It enhances emotional resilience. Happy individuals are better equipped to cope with life's challenges and setbacks. Positive emotions can strengthen the immune system, making you less susceptible to illnesses. Studies have shown that happier individuals tend to live longer.

Happy people are more likely to build and maintain strong, healthy relationships and attract others who are supportive and positive. They're more likely to show compassion and empathy, and live a harmonious existence

Other benefits are improved cognitive function, creativity, and problem-solving skills, leading to motivation and improved performance at work or school. There's a strong correlation between happiness and success in various areas of life, including career, relationships, and personal achievements.

Happiness isn't a physical existence. It's a state beyond the physical but manifests in the physical body. It resides in every being and is directly connected to the Love aspect within. Each one of us is in search of love and happiness, but instead of searching within, we're searching for it out there in material possessions, and therefore we're deprived of lifelong love and happiness.

5

THE FIVE BASIC ELEMENTS: EARTH, WATER, FIRE, AIR, AND ETHER

From earth's depth and water's grace,
To fire's spark and air's embrace,
The vast sky, a canvas wide,
In these elements, the divine resides.

The five elements, created by the divine, form the foundation of the physical universe and are the building blocks of all matter. Each element has distinct attributes and characteristics, and play a vital role in the physical, mental, and spiritual aspects of existence.

These five elements interact and combine in various proportions to form all physical matter in the universe. The balance and harmony of these elements within the body and the environment are crucial for health, well-being, and happiness.

While modern science doesn't categorize the body in terms of these five elements, there's an acknowledgment of the importance of balance in bodily functions. Concepts like homeostasis, the importance of hydration, metabolic processes, respiratory function, and our physical structure, can be seen as parallels to the traditional elements.

The following is a basic explanation of these elements.

Ether: the subtlest form of matter

Ether is the subtlest of the five elements and is omnipresent. It represents the quality of expansion and is associated with the sense of hearing. The primary attribute of Ether is sound and is the medium through which sound travels. It's infinite and provides the dimension in which all other elements exist and interact

It's believed that subtle spiritual energies and messages from higher realms traverse through the ether, connecting the individual soul with the universal consciousness. Practices like prayer, contemplation, and spiritual communion are avenues to attune yourself to this divine presence.

Air: The Breath of Life

Air is dynamic and light. It represents the quality of motion and is associated with the sense of touch, perceived through the skin.

Air is associated with life force and is vital for breathing and sustaining life. The air element signifies movement, lightness, and communication. It's the breath of life that sustains us, enabling the exchange of oxygen and carbon dioxide in our lungs. It's present in the respiratory, circulatory, and nervous system. However, it's also present in each cell of the human body. It governs the movement of thoughts, emotions, and bodily functions.

Air represents the freedom of thought and the power of communication. It encourages us to express ourselves and connect with others. In the human system, it serves as a bridge between the physical body and the mind.

It's responsible for the movement of life force energy and facilitates the communication between the physical senses and the higher faculties of perception and cognition.

Practices such as breath control, spending time in open, airy environments, and engaging in mindful communication can strengthen the air element within us, promoting mental clarity and harmonious relationships.

Fire: The Source of Transformation

Fire is radiant and intense, and represents the quality of transformation, energy, perception, and willpower.

It's also associated with the sense of sight and provides shape and visibility to objects.

It's the driving force behind our metabolism and the digestion of both food and experiences. In the human body, the fire element is evident in the digestive enzymes, metabolic processes, and body heat. It fuels our physical and mental activities, providing the energy needed to pursue our goals and passions.

On a spiritual level, fire represents the inner light of consciousness and the power of will. It's the spark of inspiration and the catalyst for personal growth and spiritual awakening.

Cultivating the fire element through practices such as sun salutations, consuming warm and spicy foods, and engaging in activities that ignite our passion, can enhance our vitality and transformative potential.

Water: The Essence of Fluidity
Water is cohesive and represents the quality of fluidity. The primary attribute of water is taste.

It's the life-giving force that circulates through our bodies, nourishing and cleansing our cells. In the human body, the water element is present in blood, lymph, and other bodily fluids, and is responsible for regulating temperature, transporting nutrients, and eliminating waste.

Spiritually, water symbolizes emotional depth and intuition. It teaches us the importance of going with the flow and adapting to the ever-changing currents of life.

Engaging in activities such as swimming, hydrating adequately, and practicing fluid movements in exercises like Tai Chi, can enhance the water element within us, fostering emotional balance and intuitive awareness.

Earth: The Foundation of Stability

Earth is dense and solid, and represents the quality of stability. It's associated with the sense of smell and is perceived through the nose. It's the foundation upon which our physical form is built, providing the strength and support needed for our bodily existence. In the human body, the earth element is manifested in the bones, muscles, tissues, and skin. These components give us the ability to move and interact with the physical world.

From a spiritual perspective, the earth element grounds us, connecting us to the physical plane and offering a sense of rootedness.

Practices such as grounding exercises, walking barefoot, and mindful eating, can help strengthen our connection to the earth element, promoting stability and resilience in both body and mind.

My personal practice:

Each day, I express gratitude to the five elements for maintaining harmony in all aspects of my physical being and restoring balance within my body whenever environmental disturbances occur.

> *"You serve the Universe, and the Universal Energy will serve you back."*
>
> *"You are One with the Source! Love your life, and the entire universe will love you back."*

6

THE HUMAN BODY: THE PHYSICAL/GROSS BODY

Earth anchors us, so firm and still,
Water nourishes with gentle will.
Fire ignites with a vibrant glow,
Air's breath makes our spirits grow.
The sky above, with its endless span,
Holds the balance of life's grand plan.

Understanding the interplay of the five elements within the human body provides a holistic approach to health and well-being. Each element contributes to our overall balance and harmony, and any imbalance can manifest as physical, mental, or emotional dis-ease. By recognizing the influence of these elements, we can take proactive steps to maintain homeostasis and overall balance.

In the context of spirituality, the human physical body is often viewed as a sacred vessel that houses the soul. It serves as a conduit through which the spirit experiences the material world. This perspective sees the body not merely as a biological entity, but as an integral part of our life journey on planet Earth.

Practices such as yoga, meditation, and mindfulness are basic tools to bring the body back to balance, so that it can continue to provide a happy nurturing state and assist in the necessities and fulfilment of the desires of the spirit body and the soul. Through these practices, we can achieve a deeper connection with the source within, facilitating the knowledge and wisdom of Oneness.

The body, in this light, becomes a vital tool for self-discovery, transformation, and the realization of our divine essence.

While the physical body anchors us to the material world, the soul and spirit elevate our existence, connecting us to higher dimensions of consciousness and purpose.

Understanding, knowing, and embracing the interplay between the physical, spiritual, and soul aspects, can illuminate the path to the ultimate love and happiness within.

7

HUMANITY: UNIVERSAL KINDNESS

In hearts that care and hands that give,
Humanity's true essence lives.
It's in the kindness we bestow,
And in the love that helps us grow.

Humanity is the quality of being human. It includes the characteristics that make us different from other creatures. These characteristics involve our ability to think, feel, and act in ways that show kindness, compassion, and understanding toward others.

At the heart of humanity is our ability to connect with each other. We form relationships and support one another. This connection is built on empathy and the desire to help those in need. When we see someone struggling, our natural reaction is often to offer a helping hand or provide comfort.

Humans are also known for their creativity and innovation. We create art, music, and literature that express our emotions and experiences.

We invent new technologies to improve our lives and solve problems. This creativity shows our drive to understand and shape the world around us.

Despite our many achievements, humanity also faces challenges. We sometimes hurt each other and make mistakes. But these difficult times remind us that being human means striving to do better and learn from our experiences. It's important to acknowledge our flaws and work towards making the world a more compassionate place.

Being human also means caring for our environment and each other. We share this planet with many other living beings, and it's our responsibility to protect and preserve it. By working together, we can create a better future for ourselves and for future generations.

In essence, humanity is about more than just existing; it's about making a positive difference. It's about understanding that each person has value and that our actions can impact others. By showing kindness, working together, and striving to improve, we embrace the true essence of humanity.

> *Ascending past the mortal plane,*
> *We seek the truth beyond the strain.*
> *In spiritual realms, our hearts align,*
> *With a higher truth, profound and divine.*

8

THE SPIRIT THE SOUL AND THE ULTIMATE SOURCE (THE DIVINE)

The soul and spirit gently blend,
In the divine's light, they find their friend.
Together they journey, hand in hand,
Guided by the divine's gentle plan.

The concepts of Soul, Spirit, and Divine are central to many religious, spiritual, and philosophical traditions, each representing different aspects of existence and the relationship between human beings and higher powers. While they're different aspects of the ONE, each has its own traits and uniqueness, and it's vital to understand the subtlety and uniqueness of each term and overcome the confusion.

The Spirit

The Spirit is often seen as the core of our individuality. It's the source of our emotions, desires, and personal identity, and carries our memories, dreams, and experiences, shaping who we are and how we relate to the world. It encompasses our emotional life, guiding us through the spectrum of feelings from joy and love, to sorrow and anger.

The Spirit, which carries imprints of all our actions and thoughts, is the reason for our passions and purpose. It represents the most transcendent aspect of our being, connecting us to the Divine and the Universal Consciousness. It's the source of our deepest wisdom, intuition, and sense of interconnectedness with the Universe, seeking to go beyond the limitations of the physical world and the Ego, while guiding us toward experiences of unity and enlightenment.

It's engaged in clearing the debris of the past, cleansing undesirable imprints that it may be carrying, and acquiring knowledge and wisdom to experience enlightenment and attain liberation. It's the spirit that travels with the imprints after death and is responsible for reincarnation and karma.

At the time of death, the Spirit and the Soul leave the physical body, as the five elements return to their original form: water to water, air to air, earth to earth, fire to fire, and ether to ether. The Spirit carries with it all of the imprints accumulated during our lifetime, while the immortal Soul remains as-is.

The Subtle Body

The subtle body refers to a complex and multidimensional aspect of human existence beyond the physical form. This energetic essence is believed to consist of several layers or sheaths that interpenetrate and interact with each other, influencing the physical, mental, emotional, and spiritual beings of an individual.

The subtle body is also believed to extend beyond the physical in the form of an aura, an electromagnetic field that surrounds and permeates the body. The aura reflects our physical, emotional, mental, and spiritual states, and can be influenced by thoughts, emotions, and energetic interactions.

At the core of the subtle body is the Life Force, often referred to as Vital Energy. Life Force is believed to flow through energy channels that run throughout the body and can be compared to the concept of meridian in Chinese medicine. It's directly related to the physiological functions, such as breathing, circulation, digestion, and the nervous system, storing the imprints of all the present and past-life experiences that haven't been cleansed or cleared.

The subtle body is progressively layered from the denser to the subtler aspects of existence. The resonance of each layer decreases with the density, with the densest being the physical layer that vibrates at the lowest frequency, and the subtlest, the causal layer, vibrating with the highest frequency.

The Physical Sheath
The physical sheath is composed of the energy aspect of the physical elements. It sustains life through physiological processes such as breathing, digestion, circulation, and sensory perception. Its attributes are stability, solidity, materiality, and interaction with the physical world.

The Vital Sheath
The vital sheath encompasses the life force and energetic processes that sustain life. It regulates the functions of the physical body, including breathing, circulation, and nervous system activities. Its attributes are movement, vitality, energy flow, and connection between the physical and energetic dimensions.

The Mental Sheath
The mental sheath encompasses the mind's activities, including thoughts, emotions, and sensory experiences, shaping mental perceptions and beliefs. Its attributes are intellect, emotions, desires, cognitive processes, and the ability to reason and discriminate.

The Intellectual/Wisdom Sheath

The intellectual/wisdom sheath is associated with higher intellect, discernment, and intuition and wisdom, facilitating deeper understanding, introspection, spiritual inquiry, and the capacity to discern truth from illusion. Its attributes are higher consciousness, spiritual insight, wisdom, discrimination, and the ability to contemplate existential questions.

The Causal Body (The Causal Sheath)

The causal body is often referred as the "body of causes". It's the deepest layer of the human aura or energy field, existing beyond the physical, emotional, and mental bodies. It's believed to house all of the present and past-life experiences, as well as the karma seeds for future actions, and is the reason for our identity, which is "this is me with my unique traits".

From a metaphysical standpoint, the causal body is the link between the individual soul and universal consciousness or Divine Existence. It represents the essence of the soul's journey across multiple lifetimes, carrying the accumulated wisdom and lessons learned through various incarnations. it's the last layer to melt away before the final unity with the Source, the Universal Consciousness/Divine Presence.

9

SPIRITUALITY

Spirituality awakens the inner sight,
A dance of the soul in eternal light.

Beyond humanity is spirituality. It's about finding a deeper meaning in life and connecting with something bigger than ourselves. It's not just about religion or specific beliefs, but a personal quest that can help us understand who we are and what gives our lives purpose.

People find spirituality in many ways. Some may connect with a higher power or God through religion, while others might find it through nature, art, music, or meditation. There are many paths to spirituality, and each person's journey is unique.

For many, spirituality is closely linked with religions like Christianity, Judaism, Islam, Hinduism, and Buddhism, as they provide a structured way to explore their beliefs by offering teachings and communities that can help people grow spiritually.

Others feel a deep connection with the natural world. The beauty of a sunset, the peace of a forest, or the vastness of the ocean can evoke a sense of awe and wonder. Nature can remind us of our place in the world and help us feel connected to all living things.

Meditation and mindfulness are practices that help us focus on the present moment. By quieting our minds, we can become more aware of the world around us, as well as our thoughts and feelings. This awareness can lead to a deeper understanding of ourselves and a greater sense of peace.

For some, spirituality is found in creative expression. Painting, writing, dancing, or playing music can be ways to connect with our inner selves and express our deepest emotions and is be a powerful way to explore and understand our spiritual nature.

Life can be tough, and spirituality provides comfort and strength during hard times, offering hope and resilience by knowing that we're part of something bigger than ourselves.

Many studies show that spiritual practices such as meditation and yoga can reduce stress, improve mood, and even boost our immune system. Connecting with others through spiritual communities also provides support and a sense of belonging.

Spirituality is a personal and unique experience that helps us find deeper meaning and connection in life. Whether through religion, nature, mindfulness, or creativity, exploring our spirituality can bring many benefits and enrich our lives. By taking the time to understand and nurture our spiritual selves, we can find greater purpose.

10

THE SOUL

The soul, pure consciousness, vast and clear,
A fragment of the divine, free from fear.
In its essence, boundless and true,
Reflects the divine in all it views.

The soul can be likened to a drop of water in the ocean, because just as it shares the same properties as the entire ocean, the soul shares the same essence as the Ultimate Divine, its source.

The Soul is often described as the true nature. It's the spark that illuminates the Subtle Body, the Causal Body, and the Gross/Physical Body and is the reason for existence. Unlike the Physical Body, which is temporary and subject to decay, and the Spirit that exists only until liberation from birth and death, the Soul never dies. It is:

- Eternal and Immortal
- Identical in essence with Divine

- Infinite in nature
- Indestructible, as it can't be destroyed by weapons, fire, water, or any physical means
- Beyond the realm of material existence
- Unaffected by the cycle of birth and Death
- the witness and observer of all experiences of the body
- infinite consciousness and bliss.
- untouched by any actions, thoughts or events that happens in the world or the body
- beyond all dualities, such as pleasure and pain, heat and cold, success and failure
- equanimous and unaffected.
- impervious to dying when the body dies.
- immobile and stays AS IS.

The essence of the Soul is as of the Divine Energy. They are always at one with each other.

The essence of the Soul is:

- unconditional Love
- bliss
- pure
- merciful
- compassion
- knowledge

- wisdom
- joy
- infinite
- calm
- peaceful
- spontaneous
- creative.

The soul is eternal, pure consciousness, identical with the supreme reality, the Divine source of all creation. It's beyond dualities and the physical realm, serving as the true self and ultimate witness. Understanding and realising the nature of the soul is essential for attaining liberation from suffering and experiencing the ultimate truth leading to love and happiness on planet Earth.

The Knowing of the Self is the spiritual journey from Ignorance to Knowledge.

To know the soul is to transcend the veil,
From ignorance to wisdom's trail.

In its depths, the truth we find,
A journey of the self to self.

"You serve the Universe, and the Universal Energy will serve you back."

"You are One with the Source!
Love your life, and the entire universe will love you back."

11

WHO AM I? THE BODY, THE SPIRIT, OR THE SOUL?

The question of identity, "Who am I?" has perplexed humanity for millennia. It's a profound inquiry that seeks to understand the essence of our being. Are we merely our physical bodies, or is there a deeper, more ethereal aspect to our existence? This chapter delves into the three interconnected dimensions of human identity: the body, the spirit, and the soul.

The Body: Our Physical Presence
The body is the most tangible and immediate aspect of our identity. It's the vessel through which we interact with the physical world and experience life. Our bodies allow us to see, hear, touch, taste, and smell, enabling us to create and explore.

Our physical form is shaped by genetics, environment, and lifestyle choices, and is subject to our mortality. While our bodies are a crucial part of our identity, they're not the entirety of who we are. They are the temporary home for our spirit and soul, allowing us to navigate the material realm.

The Spirit: Our Vital Force

The spirit is the life force that animates our bodies. It's the energy that drives our actions, emotions, and desires, as well as being the source of our creativity and intuition.

Often associated with breath or vitality, it makes us feel alive and connected to the world around us.

While the body is finite, the spirit is often perceived as more enduring. It transcends the limitations of the physical form, allowing us to experience states of consciousness beyond the ordinary.

The Soul: Our Eternal Essence

The soul is considered the most profound aspect of our identity. It's the eternal, unchanging core of who we are, beyond the physical and temporal. Many spiritual traditions describe the soul as the Divine spark within us, a fragment of the Source or Universal Consciousness.

The soul embodies our deepest values, purpose, and truth. While our body and spirit may experience turmoil and transformation, the soul remains serene and steadfast. Understanding and aligning with our soul can lead to a life of authenticity and fulfillment.

Integrating Body, Spirit, and Soul

We're not merely physical beings nor solely spiritual entities, but a beautiful amalgamation of body, spirit, and soul.

The body allows us to engage with the world, the spirit provides vitality and inspiration, and the soul offers wisdom and guidance.

Living in harmony with all three dimensions leads to a balanced and meaningful life. By nurturing our bodies, we honor our earthly existence, by cultivating our spirit, we enhance our experience of life, and by listening to our soul, we align with our highest purpose.

Embracing this wholeness allows us to live with greater awareness.

As we journey through life, let us remember that our true identity surpasses the limitations of the physical world. We're luminous beings, eternally one with the Source, embodying the infinite potential of love, happiness, knowledge, and wisdom.

While I identify myself as the Physical body,
I am thy servant. While I identify myself
as the Spirit, I am yearning for thee.
And while I identify myself as the Soul,
I am one with thee.
Hence, while on planet earth,
I am three in one.
The Body, The Spirit, and The Soul

12

THE DIVINE ENERGY: THE SOURCE OF ALL CREATION

In the divine's infinite design,
Creation's patterns intertwine.
The source of all that is and will be,
Immersed in it, we're one with thee.

Divine energy, often appearing in various spiritual traditions, is considered the fundamental life force or spiritual power that pervades the Universe. It's seen as the essence of all creation and the source of all existence.

I perceive the Divine as the limitless infinite power/energy/consciousness that we're unable to perceive yet can experience. I can only describe it as an ocean of love and mercy, manifesting according to individual perception.

Put in simpler terms, I'd say water has no shape or color of its own, profoundly takes the shape of the vessel it's contained in and reflects whatever it's mixed with.

The key attributes of Divine Energy:

- **Omnipresence:**

It pervades all things, living and non-living, and goes beyond time and space, unconfined to any place or entity. Space doesn't contain it, but the divine contains the space.

- **Omnipotence:**

It's the source of all power and capabilities in the Universe, which highlights its ability to create, sustain, and transform all forms of life and matter.

- **Omniscience:**

Is the ocean of infinite knowledge and wisdom, without limitation, encompassing past, present, and future events, including the thoughts and actions of all beings.

- **Love and Compassion:**

A nurturing and caring force that seeks the well-being and upliftment of all creation. Its benevolent and nurturing nature can be compared to unconditional motherly love.

- **Purity and Holiness:**

It's pure and holy, free from any contamination or imperfection, representing the highest form of spiritual cleanliness and sanctity, and embodying the essence of divine perfection. All contaminations get purified just by embracing it.

- **Unity and Oneness:**

Is a unifying force that connects all beings and elements of the universe, promoting the underlying oneness of all existence, harmony, and interconnectedness.

- **Transcendence and Immanence:**

Divine energy transcends all physical and material limitations, while also being inherent, meaning it exists within every part of the Universe and all aspects of life.

- **A Creative and Sustaining Power:**

Divine energy is the creative force behind the existence of the Universe, not only bringing forth creation, but also sustaining and maintaining the balance and order of the cosmos.

- **A Healing and Transformative Power:**

It heals and transforms, bringing about physical, emotional, and spiritual healing, and fostering profound personal and collective transformation.

- **Eternal and Infinite:**

It's eternal and infinite, beyond all measures and limitations, which signifies its timeless and boundless nature.

- **Peaceful and Serene:**

It's a source of profound peace and serenity, achieving calmness and tranquillity to the mind and soul.

- **Able to Provide Guidance and Wisdom:**

It provides guidance and wisdom to those who seek it, offering insight and direction, helping us navigate our spiritual life path.

- **Radiant and Luminescent:**

It's often associated with light and radiance, symbolizing enlightenment, clarity, and the dispelling of darkness and ignorance.

- **Resilient and Strong:**

The source of all that's required to overcome challenges and adversities, an enduring source of courage and success.

- **Joyful and Blissful:**

It brings a deep sense of happiness and contentment that goes beyond worldly pleasures and experiences.

The Divine Energy can be compared to a reservoir or an ocean of unlimited attributes. Knowing, understanding and embracing the true nature of the Self and the Divine leads to a harmonious, meaningful, and enlightened existence, full of love and happiness.

13

DIVINITY: LIVING IN ONENESS

In the divine's infinite design,
Creation's patterns intertwine.
The source of all that is and will be,
Immersed in it, we're one with thee.

Divinity refers to being one with the Divine Source. It is a deeply personal and profound experience that surpasses ordinary existence and spirituality, and involves recognizing our inherent unity with the source of all life, love, and wisdom.

Living in oneness with the Divine means embodying its qualities of love, peace, and compassion, and recognizing the interconnectedness of all beings. This journey leads to a life of greater fulfillment, grounded in the eternal presence of the Divine Source.

14

OCEAN OF LOVE AND HAPPINESS

In the ocean of love, we are one,
Boundless joy like the shining sun.
From this source, we find our way,
In love and happiness, we forever stay.

The Ocean of Love and Happiness is not a physical location but a profound inner experience and state of being. It represents the boundless and infinite nature of love and happiness that can be accessed through connection with the infinite and eternal nature of the Divine.

Connecting with this ocean means experiencing the oneness and unity of all existence. It pervades all creation and is the underlying reality of the Universe, full of compassion and joy.

It's available to all, without exception.

Oneness with the Ocean of Love and Happiness: The Source

Life often has limits, such as physical, emotional, and mental challenges. Recognising that we're always one with the Source helps us overcome these limits. It lets us reach higher levels of awareness and feel free and open beyond what we usually see. Being united with the Source is about finding a sense of being whole and complete, giving us a deep purpose and meaning in life, helping us see clearly and guiding us to do our work while following our dreams with love and joy.

Divinity means understanding that our true nature is one with the Divine, which is part of everything, both living and nonliving, in this Universe and beyond. By embracing this oneness with the source, we can work to bring together the different parts of ourselves and feel a deep sense of wholeness, inner peace, total fulfillment, and contentment.

Despite the wave's individuality,
it's always one with the Ocean.
So is the soul always one with
the Source, the Divine

The Ocean of Unity

Imagine being immersed in an endless ocean, its waters surrounding you, supporting you. There is no need to create water or seek it out, because it's all around you, nourishing and sustaining you effortlessly. This is what it feels like to be one with the Divine Source. When we're connected to this infinite Source, we don't need to manifest or search for the essentials of life, as they're naturally provided.

The sunlight of the Divine
Think about sitting outside on a bright, sunny day. The sunlight bathes you in its warmth and light, filling you with energy and joy. You don't need to search for the light or create it, because it's already there, enveloping you in its glow. Similarly, when we align ourselves with the Divine Source, we find that the light of understanding, wisdom, and love is ever-present, illuminating our path. We do not have to strive for it.

The cold of Mount Everest
Picture standing on the peak of Mount Everest, the highest point on Earth. The cold is intense and undeniable. You don't need to create the cold. It's simply an intrinsic part of the environment. In the same way, when we're one with the Divine Source, the qualities and blessings are naturally present in our lives. There's no need to manifest them.

The fulfilment of the desires and the necessities of Life
In this state of unity with the Source, all of our desires and necessities are fulfilled. The ocean of the Divine

provides everything we need, from love and joy, to wisdom and peace. There's no lack, no need to strive or struggle. Our deepest longings are met effortlessly, because we're one with the infinite abundance of the Source.

This has been my experience since my journey commenced. I'm surrounded by love and happiness, as if it's being radiated to me from all directions. Solutions to my issues find their way to me before the issue even arises.

In 2010, a few senior Bowen therapists approached me, seeking revision days for their continuing education.

I was surprised by their request, as I was the newest instructor, and they'd been practicing the therapy far longer than I had. Their confidence in me stirred a bit of anxiety, but I accepted their request, sensing there was a deeper reason behind it. So we scheduled their revision session for the upcoming weekend.

Just two days before the class, my clinic was broken into and ransacked. Though it was a shocking event, I remained calm, quickly reorganising the space to ensure the class could still move forward. The revision session paid $5,000, which was exactly what I needed to restore my clinic to its original condition. This experience deepened my faith in Divine love and mercy.

15

SURRENDER: EMBRACING THE OCEAN (THE SOURCE) AND LETTING GO

Surrender involves giving up control, releasing resistance, and embracing trust in a Divine Energy and its wisdom, and allowing the natural flow of life.

Surrendering our ego-driven desires and attachments helps cultivate inner peace and harmony with ourselves and the Universe. It involves letting go of the need to control outcomes and accepting things as they are, trusting the Divine will.

Trust in the Divine essence requires the strength and humility to surrender to the flow of life, including challenges and obstacles. We acknowledge our personal limitations, maintaining our trust, even in situations that are beyond our understanding.

Surrender promotes acceptance of the present moment, including its joys and challenges, allowing us to be fully present and engaged in life, without resistance or attachment to desired outcomes, finding strength in submitting to the unknown.

The rewards of surrender include inner peace, spiritual liberation, and a deep sense of connection with the Source, the Divine. It brings clarity of purpose and alignment with our true self.

Surrender can be as simple as letting go of worries, trusting intuition, and going with the rhythms of life with gratitude, or something as simple as daily rituals like mindfulness and meditation.

A newborn baby in a mother's lap:
A newborn baby embodies pure trust, as it's completely dependent on the mother for nourishment. Similarly, our surrender involves a letting go of control and opening ourselves up to the flow of life.

Babies live fully in the present moment, without concerns for the past or future, making them completely experience life as it unfolds. As adults, we can miss the beauty and mystery of the present by concentrating on regrets about the past and anxiety about the future. Mindfulness means letting go of our mistakes or any future doubts.

Just as a mother nurtures and guides her child with unconditional love, the essence of the Divine Mother guides us toward a life full of love and happiness that continues to enhance spiritual growth, inner peace, and Oneness with the Divine existence.

Building a Motherly relationship with the Divine source:

The Divine Mother represents the nurturing, compassionate, and protective aspect of the Divine. She's seen in various spiritual traditions as the ultimate source of creation, sustenance, and unconditional love. Recognizing the Divine Mother's qualities helps us align our mindset with the principles of motherly love.

The Monkey Mother:

In the thick forest, a mother monkey moves carefully from branch to branch, with her baby holding tightly to her fur, too small to climb on its own, depending completely on its mother for safety. The mother knows there's a danger of her baby falling every time she jumps or swings and becoming victim to predators, so she takes great care to balance her own movements. Her strong, protective instincts increase the close bond they share.

The Cat Mother:

The cat mother carries her kitten gently in her moth, navigating her surroundings, her powerful jaw maintaining a steady grip and providing a sense of security that allows her kitten to remain calm.

A Human Mother:

A human mother cradles her newborn baby, who's fresh into the world, completely reliant on its mother's touch and care. As the mother cleans and kisses her newborn, she marvels at the uniqueness of their bond, emotional and complex. This act of care is more than just a cleaning. It's the beginning of a lifelong bond built on unconditional love and devotion.

The Cow Mother:

A mother cow tenderly licks her newborn calf clean, removing the afterbirth and any dirt from its coat. This act of care not only cleans the calf but also stimulates its circulation and breathing. It's an essential part of the mother-calf relationship, bonding them and demonstrating the mother cow's instinctive commitment to her calf's well-being.

The Divine Mother:

The Divine Mother cradles the Universe in her embrace, gently nurturing every soul with infinite love and compassion. Just as she breathes life into existence, she also tends to the mess and chaos that arise within it, understanding that these are part of the cosmic cycle she has created. Her touch is gentle and soothing, wiping away fears and pains with a grace that transcends human understanding. In her care, every being feels a profound sense of security and peace, knowing they're cherished and protected by her boundless strength. The relationship between the Divine Mother and her creation is unique, rooted in an eternal, unconditional love that encompasses all of existence. Through her nurturing presence, she continuously renews and cleanses, guiding her children toward growth and enlightenment.

My daily conversation with the Divine source

While I identify myself as the Physical body,
I am thy servant. While I identify myself
as the Spirit, I am yearning for thee.
And while I identify myself as the Soul,
I am one with thee.
Hence, while on planet earth
I am three in one.
The Body, The Spirit, and The Soul
Surrendered to You with Love

16

SELFLESS SERVICE: THE ULTIMATE EXPRESSION OF LOVE AND HAPPINESS

The inner energetic feeling of love and happiness expresses itself in the physical as selfless service, which is a deep and powerful way to show love. It means helping others and caring about their needs more than your own, because you truly want to make a difference. It's about giving without expecting anything in return except the happiness and satisfaction you get from helping others. This compassion creates a ripple effect, inspiring others to act with love and kindness, which makes the world kinder and more interconnected.

But it's important to remember that even though selfless service is rewarding, we need to maintain balance and take care of ourselves by setting limits. However, despite the challenges, the rewards are huge when we see the effect we have on others and their success.

Nature's Unconditional Service

Nature is a remarkable teacher of selfless service. The elements of nature, such as trees, rivers, the sun, and the sky, provide essential services that sustain life on Earth. They give without expecting anything in return, serving as powerful examples of selfless love and generosity.

Trees

Trees bear fruits, flowers, and leaves. Even the trunks and roots are used by humans. They are vital to all living creatures, offering countless benefits for our environment. They absorb carbon dioxide and release oxygen, providing the air we breathe and filtering pollutants, improving air quality and promoting healthier ecosystems. Trees provide shelter and food for countless species, supporting biodiversity and maintaining balanced ecosystems.

Rivers

Rivers provide fresh water for drinking, agriculture, and sanitation, supporting human and animal life. They've historically served as pathways for trade, travel, and cultural exchange, connecting communities.

The sun

The sun is the ultimate source of energy, driving the processes that sustains us. The sun sets the natural rhythm of day and night, influencing the behaviour and biological cycles of living organisms.

The sky

The sky plays a crucial role in maintaining life and balance on Earth. It's home to the atmosphere, which regulates weather and climate, supporting diverse life forms. The sky inspires wonder and creativity, providing a canvas for stars, clouds, and natural phenomena that captivate the human imagination.

Lessons from Nature's Selfless Service

The selfless service of trees, rivers, the sun, and the sky, teaches us valuable lessons. These elements of nature give tirelessly, supporting life and inspiring us to embrace selfless service in our own lives. By recognising and valuing their contributions, we can deepen our connection to the natural world and learn to live with gratitude and respect.

> *"You serve the Universe, and the Universal Energy will serve you back."*
>
> *"You are One with the Source!*
> *Love your life, and the entire universe will love you back."*

17

CHANGE YOUR MINDSET: BE ONE WITH THE OCEAN OF LOVE AND HAPPINESS

Mindset is a powerful factor in achieving success, love, and happiness. It's the way we think and what we believe. It affects our habits, how we see problems, and how we go after our goals. There are two main types of mindsets.

1. Fixed Mindset:
People with a fixed mindset think they're either good at something or not. They might avoid challenges and give up easily.

2. Growth Mindset:
A growth mindset means believing that we can improve our abilities and intelligence with effort and learning. People with this mindset see challenges as chances to grow, keep trying when things get tough, and feel inspired by others' success.

By developing a growth mindset, we open ourselves to endless possibilities for personal and professional growth. Challenges become opportunities, failures become lessons, and learning becomes a lifelong journey.

Cultivating motherly love for the Divine Mother involves a profound shift in mindset. By developing this bond, we accept a form of love that's selfless, compassionate, and filled with devotion.

One of the key aspects of developing motherly love for the Divine Mother is humility. Recognize that, just as a mother lovingly cares for her child, the Divine Mother cares for all of creation. Through humility, we can surrender to Her guidance and protection. But this surrender isn't a sign of weakness. It's a conscious choice to trust in Her infinite wisdom and love.

These are the steps to change our perspective, enabling us to adopt a deep, nurturing connection with the Divine Mother.

1. Practice Gratitude:

Start each day by expressing gratitude for the Divine Mother's presence in your life. Acknowledge her love and protection, and thank her for the blessings she bestows.

2. Release Control:

Understand that, like a child relying on a mother, you can rely on the Divine Mother. Let go of the need to control every aspect of your life, and trust in Her plan.

Motherly love is inherently compassionate and empathetic. To develop this love for the Divine Mother, we need to enrich these qualities within ourselves. Compassion and empathy allow us to connect with others on a deeper level and see the Divine Mother in everyone.

3. Practice Loving-Kindness Meditation:
Spend a few minutes each day meditating on loving-kindness. Visualise sending love and compassion to yourself, your loved ones, and then to all beings, recognizing the Divine Mother's presence in all.

4. Perform Acts of Kindness:
Engage in selfless acts of kindness. Help those in need by offering a listening ear or simply sharing a smile. These small gestures help you to embody the nurturing qualities of the Divine Mother.

To truly develop motherly love for the Divine Mother, we need to build a personal relationship with Her. This involves spending time in Her presence, communicating with Her and opening our hearts to Her love.

5. Establish a Routine of Daily Prayer:
Establish a routine of daily prayer, where you speak to the Divine Mother as you would to a loving parent. Share your joys, fears, and desires, and seek her guidance and comfort.

6. See the Divine Mother in all that's around you:
Let Her beauty and love shine through Her creation.

As you progress to develop motherly love for the Divine Mother, you may encounter obstacles such as doubt, fear, or feelings of unworthiness.

Overcoming these obstacles requires perseverance and faith.

7. Address Doubts:
When doubts arise, remind yourself of the Divine Mother's resolute love and support. Seek answers through prayer and meditation.

8. Face Your Fears:
Recognize that fear is a natural part of the spiritual journey. Trust in the Divine Mother's protection, and take small steps to confront and overcome your fears.

9. Affirm Your Self-Worth:
Understand that you're worthy of the Divine Mother's love. Practice self-affirmations, and remember that her love is unconditional and all-encompassing.

Changing our mindset to develop motherly love for the Divine Mother is a transformative journey. By having humility, compassion, and a personal connection with her, we can nurture a deep, loving relationship that enriches our lives and brings us closer to the Divine. As we grow, we learn to see the Divine Mother's love in all aspects of life, allowing us to live with greater peace, joy, and *love our life on planet Earth*.

My daily practice:
Several times a day, I pause to feel, visualise, and immerse myself in the oneness with the Source. I constantly remind myself that everything I see, hear, feel, and taste is a manifestation of the Divine, filled with love and mercy. I believe that no one is truly wrong. Everyone is right according to their own perspective and wisdom. There's no negativity, only experiences that offer lessons or opportunities to clear accumulated debris or past imprints.

Whenever I catch my mind wandering, I engage in a gentle conversation with it, saying, "Oh, my mind..." and guide it back in my favor. This enhances my peace and harmony with my surroundings.

I know I am merely a tool, while the Divine is the doer. The doer takes care of the tool by shining and polishing it.

The story you tell yourself:
The story you tell yourself shapes your identity and influences your actions and beliefs. This internal dialogue can empower you to overcome challenges or limit you by reinforcing doubts and fears. For example, consider someone who constantly tells themselves, "I'm not good at public speaking." This belief

can lead to avoiding opportunities that require speaking in front of others, reinforcing the notion that they lack this skill.

However, by changing the narrative to "I'm learning to become a better public speaker," they open themselves up to practice and growth. This shift in mindset can lead to positive experiences, such as successfully delivering a presentation, which further reinforces their new, empowering story.

Ultimately, the way you frame your story affects your outlook on life and your ability to achieve your goals.

The story you tell yourself about spirituality and faith significantly influences your inner peace and connection to the source. If you constantly tell yourself, "I'm disconnected from the universe," this belief may lead you to feel isolated and anxious, reinforcing the idea that you're alone. However, by shifting the narrative to "I'm one with the ultimate Source," you open yourself to experiences of spiritual growth and awareness.

For example, someone who embraces the belief in their connection to a higher power might find solace in meditation, prayer, or nature, feeling a deep sense of unity and trust in their life path. This change in perspective can lead to transformative experiences, nurturing a greater sense of peace, purpose, and fulfillment.

Ultimately, the story you tell yourself about spirituality and faith shapes your ability to trust in the ultimate and embrace the mysteries of existence.

18

SILENCE AS A GATEWAY TO THE DIVINE

In stillness, spirituality unfolds,
Whispers of the divine, stories untold

Silence is often viewed as a pathway to experiencing inner stillness, which is essential for connecting with the divine presence. By quieting the mind, we become more attuned to the subtle vibrations of the divine.

Many spiritual traditions emphasize meditation, where silence is a core component. In the quiet of meditation, practitioners can transcend ordinary consciousness and access deeper spiritual insights.

In many religious traditions, contemplative prayer involves sitting in silence, allowing ourselves to be fully present with the divine. This form of prayer is about listening rather than speaking, encouraging a deeper communion with the inner voice. It enables us to listen for divine guidance, with the belief that in the absence of external noise and internal chatter, we can hear the whispers of the divine more clearly.

Silence can serve as a means of purifying the mind and spirit. By withdrawing from the constant bombarding of sensory input and distractions, we can cleanse our inner world, making space for the Divine presence.

Being in silence helps in detaching from the ego and its incessant demands, which allows us to experience a sense of unity with the Divine that's beyond personal identity and desires.

Silence represents the ineffable and mysterious nature of the Divine, surpassing human language and understanding. It points to the ultimate reality that can't be fully captured in words. The Divine presence is often felt most profoundly in moments of silence, experienced directly through the heart and soul.

Mystics from various traditions speak of achieving union with the Divine through silence. This union is characterised by a profound sense of oneness and dissolution of the individual self into the Divine. They experience a transcendental state, where ordinary reality fades away, and only the presence of the Divine remains.

Silence encourages mindfulness, allowing us to be fully present in the moment and creates a doorway to experiencing the Divine in everyday life and appreciate its timeless and accessible nature.

We can access the inner wisdom and insight that comes from a deeper connection with the Divine. Many spiritual seekers find that silence brings moments of revelation and inspiration, where new understanding and guidance emerges.

It's a means of connecting with the divine, purifying the mind and spirit, creating sacred spaces, and accessing deeper wisdom and insights. Through silence, we transcend the limitations of ordinary consciousness and feel the profound presence of the divine.

Steps to Practicing Silence

Start with a few minutes each day, and gradually increase the duration, as you become more comfortable.

1. Choose a specific time of day best suited for your lifestyle. It can be morning, during a lunch break, or before bed.

2. Select a place that has a feeling of tranquillity and where you're unlikely to be disturbed.

3. Turn off your phone, TV, and any other sources of noise or distraction. Inform others in your household that you're taking some quiet time.

4. Get comfortable in any position suitable to you.

5. Have an awareness to your breathing. Notice the inhale and exhale.

6. Let your thoughts come and go without engaging with them. Simply observe them, and let them pass.

After this practice, take a moment to reflect on how you feel.

My Personal Experience

I find answers to my questions and doubts during moments of silence. It feels like a quiet conversation with Divine energy. When someone asks me a question that I don't immediately have the answer to, my contemplation often reveals insights that amaze me.

> *In stillness, the world fades away,*
> *Revealing the divine's gentle sway.*
> *Quiet moments hold sacred grace,*
> *In serene silence, we find our place.*

CONCLUSION

Loving your life on planet Earth begins with the profound recognition of your true self, an essence that's always one with the Divine Source. This understanding transcends the illusions of separation, revealing the oneness that unites all existence. By knowing and accepting this Divine connection, you align yourself with a higher consciousness that radiates love, wisdom, and infinite possibilities. It requires a conscious shift in mindset, a deliberate choice to see the world through the lens of love rather than fear. By releasing the limiting beliefs and overcoming ignorance, we're capable of surrendering to this boundless energy of love and happiness.

As we let go of these limitations and open ourselves to the Divine flow, we experience life as a joyful journey. The ocean of love and happiness that lies within us becomes our natural state of being, where we're not merely surviving but thriving, fully immersed in the delight and abundance that comes from living in harmony with your true self. This shift in perspective allows us to navigate life with grace and ease, seeing each moment as an opportunity to deepen our connection to the Divine and to express boundless love.

Through surrender, we release our fears, anxieties, and resistance, opening our hearts to love, peace, and true contentment. This state of acceptance and trust allows us to experience life more fully, receiving each moment with gratitude and serenity.

In surrender, we find the freedom to be our authentic selves and connect deeply with the world around us, leading to a profound sense of inner fulfillment through the act of service.

*When you serve the Universe,
the Universal Source will serve you
with love.*

ACKNOWLEDGEMENTS

I'm deeply grateful to all those who've been part of the journey that led to the creation of this book. Their guidance, support, and encouragement have been invaluable.

First and foremost, I would like to express my heartfelt thanks to all of my teachers and gurus whose wisdom and insights have been a constant source of inspiration. Their teachings have profoundly shaped my understanding and have been instrumental in the development of this work.

I'm also indebted to my family and friends for their unwavering support and patience throughout the writing process. Their love and belief in me have been a pillar of strength.

Special thanks to Linda Lycett for her expert guidance and meticulous attention to detail, which have greatly enhanced the quality of this book.

Lastly, I wish to acknowledge all of the readers and fellow seekers on the spiritual path. Your curiosity and openness to explore the deeper aspects of existence are a continuous source of motivation for my work.

May this book serve as an inspiration of light on your spiritual journey and beyond.

With gratitude,
Vimla Rao

ABOUT THE AUTHOR

Vimla Rao, born and brought up in Fiji, has been a spiritual seeker from her early days. As a young scholar, she would immerse herself in scriptures, exploring their deeper meanings and insights.

Despite experiencing numerous traumas and difficulties throughout her life, Vimla never lost faith in the ultimate Source. Her struggles deepened her search, leading her to understand and embrace the Source that pervades all things, both living and non-living, in this Universe and beyond.

Having worked at various universities as a physics technical officer Vimla has an excellent understanding of the quantum aspect of the Universe.

Over the past decade, she's served as the cofounder of religious and spiritual organizations. including the Hindu Heritage Society (Sydney). She's also the founder and the director of AusHealth College of Vibrant Therapies.

Her scientific knowledge, along with her passion to know and understand life on Earth, has guided her personal journey to a level beyond ordinary perception.

Vimla has crafted a life that fulfills her needs and desires, bringing her to a place where she cherishes each moment. With over twenty years of experience in the healing industry, she's dedicated to sharing her knowledge and wisdom with those seeking love, happiness, and a life of contentment. Vimla's work continues to inspire others to connect with their own inner peace and joy.

Her mission is to help as many as possible transform themselves into a state where they happily love their Life on Planet Earth.

Vimla's message is to love all
without exception:

*"You are One with the Source!
Love your life, and the entire universe
will love you back."*

CONTACT

Email: therapist@ambienthealth.com.au
Website:
https://ambienthealth.com.au/
https://www.vibranttherapies.com/

www.ingramcontent.com/pod-product-compliance
Lightning Source LLC
Chambersburg PA
CBHW030043100526
44590CB00011B/309